Funding Your Dreams

A Guide to Personal Grants for Wealth Creation

Table of Contents

Chapter 1. Introduction

Step boldly into the world of financial independence with our Special Report: "Funding Your Dreams: A Guide to Personal Grants for Wealth Creation". This is not just a report; it's a blueprint for turning your dream of wealth and prosperity into a tangible reality. Navigate effortlessly through a myriad of personal grants, learn their nuances, and understand how best to apply them for your individual wealth creation journey. Written in an accessible, engaging style, this guide aims to demystify grant sourcing, all while injecting a healthy dose of inspiration. It's finance made incredibly exciting and achievable - a must-have for anyone desirous of funding their dreams and creating a flourishing financial future. Get ready to unleash your potential and transform your life one grant at a time!

Chapter 2. Understanding Personal Grants: The Basics

Personal grants, a somewhat elusive subject for many, represent a universe of opportunities waiting to be tapped by those who dare to dream bigger. As incentives directed towards individual endeavors, personal grants pose an essential tool in the journey towards wealth creation.

2.1. The Concept of Personal Grants

In its simplest form, a personal grant is a sum of money given to an individual – usually by a government, corporation, foundation, or trust – for a specific purpose. This money, unlike a loan, does not need to be paid back, making it an attractive prospect in wealth creation. Whether the grant supports an idea, a project, or a personal financial need, it serves as a lifeline toward realizing dreams without accruing debt.

One key detail to always remember is that grants are targeted. They are designed for a pre-decided purpose. An educational grant, for example, aims to support the costs related to schooling while an artistic grant might fund a film, a book, art installation, or other creative projects. Meanwhile, small business grants provide entrepreneurs with the financial platform necessary for turning their business ideas into profitable enterprises.

2.2. The Source of Personal Grants

Typically, personal grants are disbursed by three main types of organizations: governmental, corporate, and private foundations. Each has its unique set of grant programs crafted to realize specific objectives.

Governments - Federal, state, and local - offer grants as a means to foster initiatives in areas such as education, small business growth, agriculture, healthcare, and scientific research. They are often aimed at assisting marginalized and under-served communities, students, or struggling entrepreneurs.

Corporate grants are initiated by businesses large and small. They are usually part of a company's social responsibility program and may be focused on areas relevant to their business domain.

Private foundations, on the other hand, may support a more diverse range of categories. The funding for these grants often comes from endowments made by individuals, families, or corporations, directed toward causes close to their hearts.

2.3. Identifying the Right Grant

The first step in successfully applying for a personal grant is identifying the one that matches your unique need or project. This requires diligent research, as thousands of grants are awaiting applicants, and the ideal grant for your situations might not be the most advertised one. Websites of government entities, businesses, and private foundations are useful tools in this investigation. Alternatively, you might resort to online databases that consolidate information about available grants in all categories.

Some critical factors to consider while choosing a grant include its purpose, amount, eligibility criteria, and the stipulated usage of funds. Grant proposals that align closely with the grantor's vision and intent are more likely to be successful.

2.4. Applying for Personal Grants

Once you've identified the right grant, the next hurdle is the application process. Each grant will have an established application procedure, often involving tedious paperwork and detailed project proposals.

A well-prepared application for a personal grant should clarify how the funds will be used, prove your capability to see the project through, and demonstrate how it aligns with the purpose of the grant. Depending on the grant, you might need to present an outline of your project, a proposed budget, a timeline, personal or business financials, letters of recommendation, and any supporting credentials.

The application, while requiring considerable effort and patience, is critical to securing your desired grant. If done right, it can be the green light to your big dreams.

2.5. Grant Regulations

One must understand that grants come with regulations. There are strict stipulations on how the grant money can be used, and misappropriation of these funds can lead to serious consequences, including legal repercussions. Grant recipients are often required to submit regular reports detailing how the funds are being applied direct towards the project it was awarded for.

2.6. Conclusion

Grants enable dreams by providing financial aid without the burden of repayment. By understanding their basics, identifying your best-fit grants, and preparing diligent applications, you can access these pockets of opportunity and catalyze your journey to wealth creation.

Personal grants may not represent easy money, but they certainly represent smart money. A mastery of personal grants can be the ace up your sleeve in the game of wealth creation. Your vision could be funded by a personal grant – you need only to reach out and seize the moment.

Chapter 3. Anatomy of a Successful Grant Application

Every prosperous grant application begins with a deep understanding of its individual components and how they work symbiotically to present a compelling case to the grantor. Successful applications don't "occur" in a vacuum; they are the product of meticulous planning, research, and execution. Here, we'll dissect each element of a thriving grant application, and provide guidance on how to master each part.

3.1. Understanding the Grant and Its Purpose

The first step in creating a successful grant application is to thoroughly understand the grant and its purpose. It's crucial to study the guidelines, application form, and any other information provided by the organization awarding the grant (the grantor). Strive to understand what they are looking for, from the grant's intended purposes to the specific population or problem they want it to address. This knowledge will help you align your goals, activities, and budget with the grantor's expectations and greatly enhance the chances of your application being approved.

3.2. Knowing Your Project Inside and Out

Equally important is understanding every aspect of your own project or use for the funds. You must be able to explain your project or business goal, how the grant money will be used, and why the application aligns with the guidelines set out by the grantor. A comprehensive plan would address the following:

- What is the goal of the project or use of the funds, and how does it meet the criteria set by the grantor?

- What specific activities will be carried out?

- Who will benefit, and how?

- What is the budget for the project, and why is this amount requested?

3.3. Crafting a Captivating Proposal

A well-structured and compelling proposal is your passport to success. The proposal should tell a story about your project that captivates the reader and clearly demonstrates your capabilities and the potential benefits of funding your project. Essential elements of a great proposal are:

- Title and Abstract: These create the first impression, so make them strong, appealing, and informative.

- Goals and Objectives: What do you aim to accomplish? What measurable impacts will you have?

- Methods and Approach: How are you planning to meet the objectives? Detail your processes, strategies and methodology.

- Budget: Provide a detailed breakdown of how the grant money will be spent. Make sure the budget aligns with the proposal narrative and is reasonable and well-justified.

- Evaluation and Sustainability: Talk about how you'll track performance and measure your project's success, and how your project will be sustainable after the grant period ends.

3.4. Managing the Application Process

After creating your proposal, it's time to move onto the application itself. Many grantors provide a specific form or portal for this purpose. Be meticulous and follow their directions exactly. Fill out each section with as much detail as possible, being clear and concise. Check and double-check for errors, and be sure to submit it before the deadline.

3.5. Responding to Feedback and Rejection

Unfortunately, even the best-laid plans may encounter rejection. Even so, rejections are not entirely negative experiences. They can provide valuable feedback and are an opportunity to improve your application for the next submission. Remain tenacious, continue refining your application based on feedback and learnings, and reapply as soon as you are able.

3.6. Keeping Track and Follow-Up

Successful applicants keep a close eye on their application process. They keep track of timelines, submission dates, and any communication exchanged with the grantor. Following up on your application is also advisable, and doing so politely and courteously can demonstrate your keen interest in the grant.

To navigate the realm of grants with finesse, understanding these components will help you craft compelling narratives, present a strong case, and manage your applications effectively. By developing mastery in each of these areas, you'll be well on your way to achieving your wealth creation goals via personal grants.

Chapter 4. Exploiting Government Grants for Personal Wealth Creation

The government often provides various grants to encourage economic growth and assist its citizens in different sectors. Some of these funds can be used to facilitate personal wealth creation. This may seem an unlikely strategy for asset-building, but it is crucial to debunk this myth and explore the opportunities that exist.

4.1. Understanding Government Grants

Government grants are non-repayable funds provided by government departments, corporations, and other agencies. They are disbursed to various sectors and types of individuals for purposes ranging from scientific research to community development, education, health care and more.

The most valuable advantage of this type of funding is that they are typically 'free money.' In other words, they do not need to be repaid. However, these grants usually come with specific rules stipulating how the funds should be spent.

Knowing where and how these grants are disbursed can provide individuals with a strategic advantage. It is therefore essential to track down the sources of these grants and understand how you can apply for them.

4.2. Finding the Right Grant

Finding the right grant requires research and understanding of the government grants landscape. Following are few strategies to consider:

1. Search on Official Government Websites: Government websites are the most trusted sources to find out about available grants. Websites like grants.gov, USA.gov, or the official website of your country's finance or economic development department can be a great starting point.

2. Nonprofit Organizations and Foundations: These entities often work with government bodies and know about available grants. They can provide valuable assistance in your search.

3. Set Google Alerts: A Google alert for terms like 'government grants,' 'personal grants,' or the specific type of grant you are looking for, might yield useful information.

4. Consult with Grant Experts: There are individuals and agencies specialized in understanding and navigating the world of grants.They can provide valuable insight and advice.

4.3. Making a Successful Application

Most grant applications are detailed, requiring various forms, essays, business plans, or other documentation. Here's a step-by-step process to bolster your application:

1. **Understand the requirements**: The grant application will explicitly state the eligibility and what you must submit. Rigorously follow these instructions.

2. **Plan your Application**: A well-planned application is often more successful. Sketch out your application responses, align them with the grant's objectives, and start gathering the necessary

documents.

3. **Draft a Convincing Proposal**: Your proposal should clearly communicate how you plan to use the grant money and the expected outcomes.

4. **Review and Submit**: Review your proposal meticulously, correct any errors, and then submit before the deadline.

4.4. Maximizing Grant Opportunities

After you've secured your grant, the journey does not end there. Here's how you can maximize these opportunities:

1. **Maintain Compliance**: Ensure you comply with the stipulated grant requirements. Non-compliance could lead to penalties or even recovery of the granted funds.

2. **Regular Reporting**: Stay aligned with the grantor's reporting requirements. Timely and accurate reporting may boost your chances of securing future grants.

3. **Sustainability**: Test and implement a sustainability plan during your grant period. The goal is to build systems that persist and grow even after the grant period.

4.5. Conclusion

Government grants are a formidable yet often overlooked tool for personal wealth creation. By understanding the intricacies, finding the right grant, and making winning applications, you can harness their potential. Meanwhile, it's crucial to maximize these opportunities to ensure sustained wealth creation beyond the grant period.

Securing a government grant is not a sprint but a marathon. It needs patience, critical understanding, and persistence. Embrace the journey, and inch closer to your financial independence, one grant at a time.

Chapter 5. Venturing into Private Sector Grants

The private sector often holds untapped funding opportunities, ripe for the ambitious dream-weaver. A varied landscape filled with traditional businesses, start-ups, and corporations large and small, the private sector regularly allocates funding for a multitude of purposes including research, product development, and entrepreneurship. Private sector grants, while competitive, are a viable and often substantial means through which individuals can foster wealth creation.

5.1. Understanding the Private Sector Landscape

Private sector institutions are not duty-bound to provide grants as their government counterparts are. Such funding opportunities are often part of corporate social responsibility (CSR) programs or stem from their strategic interest. Understanding the landscape of private sector grants entails in-depth knowledge of the differing interests, focus areas, and objectives of innumerable businesses. This understanding can dramatically increase success rates in grant applications as you learn to align your interests with that of potential grantors.

5.2. Research Your Potential Grantors

Begin with creating a comprehensive list of potential grantors. Look for businesses within your sector or showing interest in your domain. Usually, large corporations have specific grant programs. Moreover, many have dedicated CSR departments providing grants in diverse areas such as education, technology, health, and the environment.

After establishing a list, delve into each corporation's grant scheme. Research not just their focal points, but also the type of projects they have funded in the past. Understand their evaluation criteria and ultimate objectives. Building a clear picture of potential grantors can help tailor a grant proposal that strategically aligns with their interests.

5.3. Crafting Your Grant Proposal

The broad diversity in the private sector commands a flexible and innovative approach to crafting your grant proposal. This section will guide you through the crucial elements of developing a proposal that stands out.

First, articulate a clear, compelling vision of your project or business. Discuss how it contributes positively to society, aligns with the grantor's objectives, and outlines the long-term sustainability or growth plan.

Present a detailed budget outlining where you will use the funding. Including specifics makes your proposal more credible and helps the grantor see how their funds will aid your project.

Finally, demonstrate your project or idea's viability. This aspect could include market research, project timelines, or proven piloting efforts if any. Rounding off your proposal with these substantiating details can establish the authenticity and viability of your project to your potential grantors.

5.4. Staying Resilient in the Face of Rejection

The quest for private sector grants is a journey rife with competition and potential rejection. Being resilient is key. Stay optimistic, tenacious, and determined. Remember that every rejection is one step closer to your successful grant proposal. Learn from missteps and feedback to refine your strategy and improve future proposals.

A steadfast and methodical approach to grant-seeking can yield significant benefits in the long run. Analyze the evaluation feedback from your grantors to make revisions and enhance your proposal. Moreover, it bolsters your relationships with potential grantors and increases the odds of achieving future funding success.

5.5. Building Relationships in the Private Sector

Strong relationships with grantors are potentially valuable assets in the journey towards financial independence. Beyond the immediate advantage of securing funding, establishing trusted partnerships can offer you strategic advice, mentorship, and access to extended networks.

Proactively engage with potential grantors through networking events, industry seminars, and social platforms. Leveraging your networks could mean the difference between a forgotten application and the beginning of a solid partnership.

Investing time in cultivating relationships, while eventually beneficial, can be an intensive process. However, the relationships you build with the private sector can unlock access to knowledge, expertise, and further potential funding avenues leading to sustained wealth creation.

In summary, navigating the realm of private sector grants necessitates thorough research, strategic alignment of interests, innovative proposal crafting, resilience, and relationship building. Despite the challenges, with persistence and savvy navigation, you stand to acquire substantial funds and immerse yourself in partnerships that support your wealth creation journey. Through careful preparation and the right mindset, you can turn the daunting quest for private grants into an opportunity-filled adventure towards abundant financial independence.

Chapter 6. Achieving Dreams through Educational Grants

Education has always been heralded as the key to unlocking individual potential and offering the promise of improved financial standing. It is, therefore, no surprise that our journey to financial independence begins with educational grants. These present an immensely viable path to wealth creation, unimpeded by the often crippling burden of college loans and extended periods of indebtedness. Let's delve deeper into how you can harness the power of educational grants to fund your dreams and foster a prosperous future.

6.1. Untangling the Complex World of Educational Grants

Educational grants are non-repayable funds provided by a granter, typically a government department, corporation, foundation, or trust, to a recipient, usually (but not always) an educational institution, scholar, or an individual researcher. Grants may cover tuition costs, funds for living and transportation, research, and more, and are given on the basis of various criteria - student need, academic merit, or particular fields of study.

Understanding the various types of educational grants is your first step towards leveraging them effectively. Some common types include federal grants, state grants, school grants, and special-interest organization grants. Federal and state grants are often need-based, school grants may be both need and merit-based, and special-interest organization grants can be based on a myriad of factors including ethnicity, gender, field of study, or even personal hobbies.

6.2. Identifying the Right Educational Grants

The key to success here lies in identifying grants that align with your individual situation, skills, and aspirations. Start with your intended field of study. Numerous grants are available for students planning to pursue major in-demand fields such as healthcare, education, and social work.

A comprehensive analysis of your financial situation is crucial too. For students with compelling financial need, programs such as the Federal Pell Grant offer substantial aid. Meritorious students may find grants that reward academic excellence or outstanding abilities in areas such as sports or the arts.

Remember, your demographic data can also serve as a grant access point. Numerous grants are geared towards specific groups such as veterans, minorities, or women. Be thorough and consider all aspects of your personal context - you may be eligible for more grants than you realize.

6.3. Mastering the Application Process

Now that you have identified potential grants, focus on submitting strong applications. Each grant will have its unique application process and criteria. Take the time to understand these requirements and align your application accordingly. Put effort into clearly outlining your objectives, aspirations, and the reasons why you should be awarded the grant.

Don't overlook the importance of presenting a compelling personal narrative. Educators and grant committees appreciate authenticity and passion - showcase yours. If a grant involves a personal statement or essay, use it as a platform to clearly articulate how the grant aligns with your long-term goals and how it will help achieve them.

6.4. Leveraging Educational Grants for Wealth Creation

It is important to understand how receiving an educational grant aids in wealth creation. First, by significantly reducing or eliminating college tuition, you are bypassing years of potential debt from student loans. This frees up capital that you can then channel into investments and wealth accumulation much earlier than your debt-burdened peers.

Moreover, the education you gain courtesy of these grants opens doors to well-paying jobs and promising careers, setting you on a path towards financial independence. Some grants, particularly those for research, may also lead to patents or entrepreneurial ventures, both of which bring lucrative opportunities.

6.5. Conclusion: From Learner to Earner

As with any journey, the road to wealth creation through educational grants requires effort, research, and persistence. But with the debt-free education these grants offer and the strong foundation they provide for future earnings and investments, the rewards far outweigh the effort involved. So delve in, harness the power of educational grants to fund your education, fuel your dreams, and transform your financial future.

Chapter 7. Stepping Stones of Success: Small Business Grants

The journey to business success often begins with a single step: finding the necessary funding. It's a matter of connecting with the right resources and extending reach where others fail to even look. Among the most underutilized of these resources are small business grants. These are non-repayable funds given by one party, often a government department, corporation, foundation, or trust, to a business. Most grants are awarded to businesses who attempt to advance social, scientific, technological, or other types of causes.

7.1. What Are Small Business Grants?

Small business grants are free money, typically distributed by government entities, private companies, or non-profit organizations, that you don't have to pay back. Unlike business loans, you don't incur debt or have to repay with interest. The intention is to financially assist small businesses, especially those that are in sectors or geographical locations that are prioritized for development, those led by underrepresented communities, or those advancing projects with potential social or economic benefits.

However, these grants are often tied to specific requirements or objectives. The grantor seeks to foster development in a particular area or industry, thus making it necessary for businesses to align their goals with those grantors' objectives.

7.2. Why Seek Small Business Grants?

The most apparent reason to seek a small business grant is the financial help it provides, particularly at the early stages of a business when budgeting may be tight. This funding can pay for equipment, inventory, marketing efforts, hiring staff, and other expenses that may otherwise strain a new business's cash flow.

Grants not only relieve financial pressure but also generate added value. Being selected for a grant usually implies some form of validation, which can enhance your business's credibility in the eyes of prospective customers, partners, and investors.

7.3. How to Find the Right Grants?

There are several ways to find grants suitable for your small business, but it requires some homework.

Firstly, check government websites. Both federal and state governments offer grants for small businesses. Some grants might have specific objectives, for example, supporting innovation or boosting the economy in an underdeveloped region. The government's goal is to stimulate economic activity and job creation, so look for programs that align with this.

Corporate grants are another option. Many big companies have corporate social responsibility programs that give back to the community. Often, these grants aim to provide opportunities for minority-owned enterprises or businesses in specific sectors.

Non-profits and associations can also provide grants. Many industry associations, local chambers of commerce, or foundations offer grants with goals ranging from stimulating economic activity in the local area to fostering industry innovation.

Regular online research, grant database subscriptions, and networking are essential for finding the right funding sources.

7.4. Applying for a Small Business Grant

Applying for a grant can be challenging. Most grantors require detailed proposals. They look for a strong business plan, a clearly defined project or initiative, a realistic budget, accomplished team, and often a commitment to social responsibility or job creation.

The application process may also require time-intensive components like market research reports, financial statements, and a detailed explanation of how the money will be spent.

Ensure your application stands out by thoroughly researching the grantor's priorities, understanding their objectives, and aligning your proposal accordingly.

7.5. Making the Most of Your Grant

Upon receiving a grant, the work doesn't stop there. Managing and making the most out of your grant is just as vital as getting it. Firstly, ensure to thoroughly understand the stipulated terms on grant usage and adhere stringently to them, as misappropriation often results in severe penalties.

Also, maintain clear financial records indicating how the grant money was spent. Regular financial audits might be a part of the award agreement. To anticipate these, systematically record expenses tied to the grant with precise documentation for each.

Lastly, the reinvesting profits back into your business can propel you one step closer to a flourishing financial future.

7.6. Success Stories

Take heart from those who have done it successfully before. Learning from others' experiences and emulating their strategies can significantly ease your grant seeking process.

For instance, "Alex and Ani," a jewelry brand started with a small business grant and transformed into a business that generated over $1 billion in sales. In another instance, mobile app development company "AI Factory," funded with a grant, went on to develop successful apps for Android.

While finding and applying for business grants can be daunting, they represent an opportunity that's just too valuable to ignore. Leverage these resources, and take another critical step towards your dreams of wealth creation.

Chapter 8. Fine-tuning Techniques for Grant Research

As we embark on the quest of grant sourcing, the first step we encounter is the research phase. This initial step might sound trivial, yet it is the cornerstone upon which the entire grant application process is premised. It is analogous to building a house: the research phase is the foundation, and the grant application is the house itself. A properly conducted research phase assures that the subsequent steps unfold smoothly and increase the likelihood of a positive outcome in the grant application process.

8.1. Begin with a Self-Evaluation.

You should start by introspectively contemplating your project, idea, or organization. Ask yourself what your mission is, who could potentially be interested in funding your project, what you want to achieve, and how much funding will be needed. Review your project with a lens of realism and pragmatism; ensure that your idea or organization has a solid foundation, a clear objective, and a well-defined path. Defining your needs before searching for a grant will help you navigate effortlessly through the myriad funding opportunities available and avoid wasted time pursuing unfit grants.

8.2. Explore Various Sources for Grant Information.

Grants can be sourced from numerous places: governmental agencies, private foundations, educational institutions, and corporations. Each has its unique way of advertising and disbursing the grants, and therefore, a keen understanding of how to mine information from each source is essential. Avail yourself of every opportunity offered by these channels. Here are a few specific platforms to consider in your research:

1. *Grants.gov*: This comprehensive database maintained by the U.S. federal government lists all federal funding opportunities. This valuable resource should be bookmarked by every serious grant researcher.

2. *Foundation Directory Online (FDO)*: FDO is a database of private philanthropic funding sources in the United States, which provides information about grantmakers and their grants. It offers a wealth of information about private grants and could be an excellent place to seek funding.

3. *Local and Regional Foundations*: Don't underestimate the value of local funding opportunities. Many communities have local foundations that are looking to invest in projects benefiting their area.

4. *Specialized Databases*: Certain sectors have databases particularly dedicated to them. For example, in the field of education, sites like *Grants Alert* and *GetEdFunding* can be incredibly valuable resources.

8.3. Develop a System for Organizing Grants.

The process of searching for grants can produce an overwhelming amount of information. For this reason, developing a systematic way of organizing the information collected is not just useful, it's critical. This can be as simple as a spreadsheet that catalogs grant names, so you don't lose track of the ones you've researched, deadlines of the grants, eligibility criteria, and information that has to be included in each application. This system will help prevent any mishaps during the application phase.

8.4. Understand the Nuances of Each Grant.

Every grant is unique in its requisites, terms, and conditions. Deciphering who qualifies, what the fund covers, when to apply, and how to apply can be daunting. Spend time perusing the grant guidelines, prerequisites, and eligibility criteria. A close examination will prevent the application from being rejected on some technical ground. Some grants may only fund non-profit organizations; others may focus solely on individuals; yet others will specify what the funds can be used for, whether it's startup costs, operational costs, or educational expenses. Understanding these nuances will allow you to apply to the right grants and increase your chances of success.

8.5. Refine Your Research Over Time.

Your research process should not be static, but rather a dynamic, evolving process. As you uncover more information and gain more experience searching for grants, you will begin to identify critical details you may have initially overlooked. Continually refining your research methodology will lead to better results in the long run.

The road to grant acquisition can often feel arduous and convoluted, but persistently fine-tuning your research process will ultimately pave your journey towards financial independence. After you've mastered the fine art of grant research, you'll be well on your way to funding your dreams and creating a flourishing financial future. Remember, as with any endeavor, the more dedicated effort you put in, the more outstanding results you yield. Be patient, be methodical, and above all, maintain resolute passion and faith in your mission.

Your dream is within reach!

Chapter 9. Personal Narrative and Its Role in Grant Proposals

The story you weave about yourself and your ambitions plays a pivotal role in determining if your grant proposal will secure funding. Let's delve into the significance and procedure of constructing an impactful personal narrative for your grant proposal.

9.1. Crafting Your Personal Narrative

A personal narrative is an intimate account of an individual's life history and personal experiences. It is a powerful tool used to communicate your passion, resilience, and core values that can create empathy and an emotional bond with your prospective grantors. During your grant proposal's drafting process, effectively incorporating your individual storyline can add a poignant touch to your appeal.

Your personal narrative should include the driving factor that motivates your project, your experiences, and the obstacles you have had to overcome. This can build credibility and demonstrate your commitment to your proposed project.

Consider these pointers:

1. Share your inspiration or reason behind initiating your project.
2. Talk about your lived experiences and how they relate to your venture and the funding needed.
3. Remember to be authentic, credible, and truthful.

The crafting of your narrative is a strategic process. You must strike a balance between being emotionally poignant, while remaining factual and focused on your project's goals.

9.2. Incorporating Your Narrative Into the Grant Proposal

Your personal narrative can be incorporated seamlessly throughout your grant proposal. Here's how:

1. Executive Summary: Briefly introduce your personal narrative, presenting a snapshot of who you are, your motivations, and what you hope to achieve.

2. Organizational Description: Weave your narrative into your organization's journey, demonstrating how your experiences have informed the work you do.

3. Needs Statement: Use your narrative to paint a picture of the problem this grant will help solve.

By strategically integrating your personal narrative in these sections, you not only showcase your deep commitment but also portray how you connect to the greater purpose behind the grant.

9.3. Engaging the Reader through Personal Narrative

A compelling personal narrative has the power to keep the reader engaged and invested in your story. It is the difference between a cold, mechanical proposal and one that resonates on a human level.

Yet, writing a captivating personal narrative can be challenging. It requires structure, creativity, and detail. To keep the narrative engaging:

1. Infuse your narrative with a touch of drama: This doesn't mean exaggeration. Rather, depict real-life situations that exemplify your passion, resilience, or determination.

2. Showcase your unique perspectives and experiences: Your individual experiences make your narrative unique and help contextualize your proposal and funding needs.

3. Be reflective: Provide insights about what you've learned from your experiences, and how these learnings will influence the successful execution of your project.

Always remember to keep your narrative concise and to the point. The reader should be able to understand your central message clearly.

9.4. The Ethos of Personal Narratives

In the context of a grant proposal, your personal narrative serves as your chance to not only introduce yourself to the grantor but also to demonstrate your ethos. The ethos—your credibility or character—acts as an authority in your proposal.

Your ethos can help build trust between you and your readers, assuring them of your capability and dedication. It can also illustrate your alignment with the grantor's values and goals, increasing the chances of your proposal's approval.

Your personal narrative is a stepping stone towards your financial independence. It tells your story, conveys your ideals, reinforces your credibility, and helps build a connection with your potential grantors. Through this intimate recounting of your journey, you foster an emotional bond that can prove to be a deciding factor in securing your personal grant.

Chapter 10. Mastering the Follow-up: Beyond the Application

The acquisition of grants is not a single encounter event; rather, it's a well-choreographed series of interactions. The submission of a grant application is only part of the process. What you do after submitting it can significantly influence the outcome. Mastering the art of post-application engagement, or the 'follow-up,' is critical.

10.1. Understanding the Follow-up

At its core, a follow-up is a professional mode of communication, intended to keep your application at the forefront of the grantor's mind. It provides an opportunity to show your initiative, passion, and commitment towards your proposed dream or project. Furthermore, it can also help establish a rapport with the grantor, potentially setting the stage for future opportunities.

Now, it's crucial to know when, how, and how often to follow-up. Every grantor organization or individual counts on different guidelines, and it is vital to adhere to these in your follow up to elicit a positive response.

10.2. Timing of the Follow-ups

Timing is a critical factor in the follow-up process. Following up too soon, too frequently, or too late, can leave a negative impression about your professionalism and judgment.

Typically, it is advisable to give grantors at least one to two weeks after your application submission before sending a follow-up email or making a call. This period is to ensure that the grantor organization has time to process your application.

However, each grantor could differ in their processing times, priorities, and schedules. Hence, it is always wise to ask during the application stage on the best timeframe to follow-up.

10.3. The Follow-Up Channels

Most popular modes of communication for follow-ups include emails, phone calls, or physical letters. The choice of your follow-up channel should align with the grantor's preferences or the communication means utilized during the application process.

Emails: Email is a popular method for follow-ups due to its non-intrusive nature, giving the grantor the flexibility to reply at their convenience. However, ensure your email is concise yet effective. Subject line matters as it should grab attention but also portrait professionalism.

Phone Calls: A direct call can often facilitate more immediate feedback. However, it's imperative to make sure that you remain respectful of the grantor's time and schedule the call at their convenience.

Letters: Some may deem it old-fashioned, but a neatly composed physical letter of follow-up sent through registered post can communicate a high level of professionalism and seriousness. Always maintain a formal tone, and don't forget to enclose a copy of your grant application for reference.

10.4. Follow-Up Content

Your follow-up communication should serve to reinforce your proposal's merit and your dedication to it, sprinkled with a respectful dose of urgency. It should consist of:

- A polite reminder about your grant application
- A brief reinforcement of why your proposal is worthy of the grant
- An acknowledgment of the grantor's time spent in reviewing your application
- A request for any updates or feedback pertaining to your application

10.5. Managing the Response

Responses to follow-ups vary. In several cases, you may not receive a reply right away, or the feedback might not be what you expected.

Silence: If your follow-up receives no reply, wait a reasonable period before sending another follow-up, usually a week. Remain persistent but professional.

Rejection: If your application has been rejected, pay attention to the reason for rejection if given. It's also worth the effort to ask for feedback or areas for improvement for your future applications.

Success: if your application is successful, make sure to send an acknowledgment, expressing your gratitude promptly.

10.6. Building a Rapport

Establishing a good relationship with the grantor can be beneficial for future grant applications. Even if your application wasn't successful, maintaining a courteous and professional demeanor, seeking advice, and displaying a willingness to adapt and improve can leave a positive impression and open doors in the future.

Monitoring deadlines and important dates, remembering names, and understanding the grantor's work will strengthen your rapport and set you apart from other applicants.

Acquiring grants is a rigorous process, and mastering the follow-up can be a powerful tool at your disposal to secure funding for your dream. When utilized correctly, it can make the difference between funding your dreams or falling short. Remember, the true art of successful grant follow-up lies in blending professionalism, understanding, persistence, and respectful communication.

Chapter 11. Nurturing Wealth with Endowment Grants: Unique Strategies for the Long Run

Endowment grants are a treasure trove often overlooked in one's wealth creation journey. These grants usually originate from foundations or trusts, traditionally to support non-profit organizations in their developmental activities or research endeavors. However, it is a little-known fact that they can also be used by savvy individuals to fortify their wealth acquisition strategy. Despite their potential, leveraging endowment grants requires a deep understanding of their nuances, eligibility criteria, and application procedures.

11.1. Understanding Endowment Grants

In essence, an endowment grant is a long-term investment in your financial prosperity. Foundations create these grants with an underlying capital base, which is not spent but invested to generate annual income. This income, known as the endowment, is then distributed as grants.

Understanding the framework within which these are operated is crucial. Unlike other grant types, endowment grants are usually linked to long-term outcomes, often rewarding persistence, vision, and an ardent commitment. Typically, these grants focus on areas like education, entrepreneurial efforts, research, arts, environment, and health.

11.2. Harnessing Potential: Identifying Grant Opportunities

Taking the first step towards leveraging endowment grants is identifying the right grant opportunity that aligns with your wealth creation goals. Start by understanding which areas of funding that foundations tend to support, as this can provide immediate insight into potential endowment grant opportunities.

Look out for foundations focused on areas that align with your vision or targets. For instance, if you are eyeing entrepreneurial wealth creation, seek out foundations supporting startups or small businesses.

Chapter 12. The Unique Power of Research Grants

Research grants are typically associated with academia, but they are also open to independent researchers and entrepreneurs. Expanding one's horizons and not confining oneself to traditional avenues can truly unlock the potential of research grants. A technology startup, for example, might significantly benefit from a research grant designed to nurture innovation in a specific sector, thus promoting wealth generation.

12.1. Navigation and Matching: Choosing the Right Grant

Once potential grants have been identified, one needs to match these opportunities with personal financial goals. This step involves comparing grant requirements, prospective gains, and tactical fits. Since endowment grants usually entail long-term commitment, it is crucial to ensure that your choice aligns perfectly with your wealth creation strategy over time.

12.2. Application: Crafting a Masterpiece

A winning application for an endowment grant is akin to crafting a masterpiece. It should effectively communicate your vision, demonstrate the potential for achievement, and substantiate your claim with evidence of past accomplishments and future plans.

Ensure that you meet all eligibility criteria and submit all the required documents, outlining your roadmap, objectives, and milestones. Strong grant proposals also exhibit potential for scalability, sustainability, and broad impact, alongside a clear understanding of the challenges ahead and how to navigate them.

12.3. Nurturing Relationships: The Secret Sauce

Successful grant applications are often the result of nurtured relationships with grantmaking bodies. Proactive communication before and during the application process can increase your chances of success significantly. Ensure to engage with the foundations, update them on your progress, attend any events that they host and affirm your commitment towards your shared goals.

12.4. Turning Rejection into Opportunity

If your endowment grant application is declined, use this as an opportunity to learn, adapt, and improve. Request feedback, reflect on where your proposal might have fallen short, and use these insights to strengthen future applications. Remember, resiliency is the cornerstone of wealth creation; more often than not, success follows numerous iterations and refinements.

12.5. Making the Most of the Grant: Nurturing Wealth

Once received, the grant must be utilized effectively and consciously to nurture wealth. Regular monitoring, financial planning, and shrewd investment are integral components to maximize the gains from an endowment grant.

Endowment grants, with their capacity for realizing significant long-term profit, represent an overlooked avenue in the journey towards financial independence. Navigating the complexities of this process might seem daunting at first, but with dedication, commitment, and strategic planning, the rewards could be unrivaled. Your dream of creating and nurturing your wealth can find a robust foundation in endowment grants. Be patient, persevere, and prepare to prosper!

www.ingramcontent.com/pod-product-compliance
Lightning Source LLC
Chambersburg PA
CBHW062312290526
45794CB00006B/2779